D0734815

Encouragement
for an
Exceptional
Life

Encouragement for an Exceptional Life

VICTORIA OSTEEN

FaithWords

NEW YORK · NASHVILLE

FaithWords
Hachette Book Group
1290 Avenue of the Americas, New York, NY 10104
faithwords.com
twitter.com/faithwords

First Edition: April 2021

FaithWords is a division of Hachette Book Group, Inc. The FaithWords name and logo are trademarks of Hachette Book Group, Inc.

The publisher is not responsible for websites (or their content) that are not owned by the publisher.

The Hachette Speakers Bureau provides a wide range of authors for speaking events. To find out more, go to www.hachettespeakersbureau.com or call (866) 376-6591.

Unless otherwise noted, Scripture quotations are taken from The Holy Bible, New International Version®, NIV®. Copyright ©1973, 1978, 1984, 2011 by Biblica, Inc.™ Used by permission of Zondervan. All rights reserved worldwide. www.zondervan.com. The "NIV" and "New International Version" are trademarks registered in the United States Patent and Trademark Office by Biblica, Inc.™

Scripture quotations noted NLT are taken from the Holy Bible, New Living Translation, copyright © 1996, 2004, 2007 by Tyndale House Foundation. Used by permission of Tyndale House Publishers, Inc., Carol Stream, IL 60188. All rights reserved.

Scripture quotations marked NKJV are taken from the New King James Version®. Copyright © 1982 by Thomas Nelson. Used by permission. All rights reserved.

Scripture quotations noted AMP are taken from The Amplified Bible. Copyright © 2015 by The Lockman Foundation, La Habra, CA 90631. All rights reserved. For permission to quote information visit www.lockman.org.

Scripture quotations noted AMPC are taken from The Amplified Bible Classic Edition. Copyright © 1954, 1958, 1962, 1964, 1965, 1987 by The Lockman Foundation, La Habra, CA 90631. All rights reserved. For permission to quote information visit www.lockman.org.

Library of Congress Control Number: 2020951070

ISBN: 978-1-5460-1787-5 (hardcover); 978-1-5460-1805-6 (ebook)

Printed in the United States of America

LSC-C

Printing 1, 2021

CONTENTS

INTRODUCTION

When something is exceptional, it means that it is better than good; it is outstanding. The exceptional stands out from the crowd, is extraordinary, and is something to be celebrated. You were made by God to be exceptional.

Scripture says you are God's masterpiece, formed in His image, and created to do great things. You were wonderfully made, with a purpose and a destiny that is distinctly yours. God knew you before you were born, and He designed you to be you, unique and exceptional.

But too often we lose sight of who God made us to be. We don't recognize the individual gifts and talents that God has placed in us. If we're not careful, we can allow our God-given attributes to be reduced in our own minds, causing us to see ourselves as merely average, mediocre, or mundane.

When I think about the challenges and difficulties I've faced in my life, there were times when I would become discouraged and ask myself, *Is this worth it? Does it even matter?* But I've realized that when I press through the challenges with faith, I discover the exceptional qualities God has placed in me, and I learn valuable lessons. When I am willing to take steps of faith and place them in God's hands, that's when the exceptional in me is produced.

I've noticed that when I put certain practices in place and incorporate them in my life, I feel myself stepping into my exceptional self each and every day. I've written this book to show you seven practices that keep me reaching for the exceptional. My hope is that you use these practices to be encouraged, empowered, and inspired in your life.

I pray this book will be a blessing for you. That these practices lead you closer to God and nearer to who He made you to be. You are fearfully and wonderfully made.

Live this truth today: You are Exceptional.

Know That You Are Chosen

I have a good friend named Jim, who I've known for many years. Jim told me a story one day that has stayed in my heart ever since. It's the story of when he met his baby sister for the first time. Jim was eight years old. He had been an only child for quite some time, and he was incredibly excited about having a sister. Finally the day came when his father showed up at school and took him out of class to head to the hospital. As his father drove through the streets of the town, parked in the parking lot, and then walked Jim down the long hallways of the hospital, Jim's stomach was rumbling with anticipation. They came to a stop in front of a large nursery window. Jim peered through the glass and saw rows of little babies all bundled up like burritos in their bassinets. A nurse looked up and recognized Jim's father. She smiled and walked out of the nursery, right up to Jim, and bent down to his level. She put her hand on his shoulder and said, "That's your baby sister right there," as she pointed out which baby belonged to his family. As Jim saw her for the first time, his face lit up with joy. There, at last, was his baby sister.

Later that day, recognizing how meeting his sister had made such a strong impression on his son, Jim's father decided to tell Jim about the day that he was born. He sat down on the sofa right next to his precious boy. He looked into his eyes, making sure he had Jim's full attention, and said, "Jim, when you were born, your mother and I looked through a large nursery window at all the babies, kind of like you and I did today. But something different happened. The nurse told us, 'You can have any baby in this nursery that you want.' We looked at all those babies and we chose you."

You see, Jim is adopted. He didn't know it until that moment. But his father wanted to communicate something very important that day. He wanted him to know this truth: "Jim, you were chosen to be our son. You are so valuable and important to us that we handpicked you to be a part of our family."

Throughout his life, Jim's father always made sure Jim knew how much he was loved and how grateful they were that he was in their family.

That is what your Heavenly Father wants you to know today. You are chosen. Ephesians 1 describes God's great love for you. It says that before the foundation of the world, it pleased God to adopt you as His very own child. He looked through the corridors of time and knew you by name. He handpicked you and brought you into His family through Jesus Christ. He didn't have to adopt you. God chose to adopt you because it pleased Him to call you His own.

Jim's father would often tell him, "Jim, you were chosen. Don't let anyone tell you any different."

Just like Jim's father reminded him, you need to get up every day and remind yourself that the Creator of the universe chose you and you are valuable to Him. Don't let your mistakes, failures, or other people talk you out of who you are.

Life has a way of trying to bring us down, discount us, and cause us to forget our true identity. People may judge us, leave us out, and make us feel unqualified. None of that determines who you are—God has already called you and qualified you. You may have made some mistakes. We all have, but that doesn't change your value in the eyes of God. He loves you. Not because of your performance, not because you do everything perfectly, but because you are His child. Take off the negative labels and let go of what people have said to you. Quit beating yourself up for things you can't change. God wants you to move forward in faith, believing that you are chosen, exceptional, and well able to do what He has called you to do.

Know Who You Are

When King David was a young shepherd boy, he was out in the fields tending his father's sheep when the prophet Samuel came to his house to anoint the next king of Israel. Jesse, David's father, brought in all seven of David's older brothers and had them stand in front of Samuel, saying, "Take a look at these fine young men. I believe the king is here." Samuel looked at those tall, strong men and said, "Jesse, the king is not here. Are these all the sons you have?"

I can hear Jesse saying, "Well, there is still the youngest, but he is tending the sheep." Perhaps Jesse didn't think that David was old enough or strong enough to be chosen by God to be king. But when David walked in from the fields, the Lord said to Samuel, "Rise and anoint him. He is the one."

Can you imagine how David felt when he walked in the house and saw all his brothers were first choice and he came in last? David could have been offended, thinking, *Why didn't my dad even consider me?* He could have been upset at the thought of being over-looked or put his head down, thinking, *I guess nobody believes in me. Why should I believe in myself?*

But David didn't have that attitude. He decided, *If I am chosen to be king, I am going to believe that I am a king.* God had already chosen David to be king of Israel long before he was tending his father's sheep out in the fields. Just because David's father didn't recognize the calling on his life didn't change the fact that he was already chosen. His family might have counted him out, but God had already counted him in. They didn't think he looked like the next king. He was too young; he didn't have the training or experience.

But God knew what was inside of David. God also knows what's inside of you, because He put it there. He knows what you're capable of. If you have ever felt the sting of rejection like David, remember who you are. You are called and chosen by God. Nothing disqualifies you from God's plans, not even a father who doesn't believe in you. Your family may not see your potential, you may not feel appreciated, people at work may not recognize your gifts and talents, friends may leave you out, but don't get discouraged. Like David, God sees you, He knows exactly where you are, and He is calling you in. No one can take your place. Nothing has the power to change God's plan for your life. Don't let other people's actions cause you to question what God has placed inside of you. Stand up tall; God's hand is on your life. He has chosen you to do great things.

God being for you is more powerful than the world being against you.

To be exceptional, you have to know who you are and Whose you are. Now, just because you've been chosen doesn't mean everything happens right away. There is often a period of waiting required. Those times of waiting can be hard. You may feel as though you're out in the shepherds' field today. Don't give up because of challenges or obstacles you may be facing.

After David was anointed king, it took him thirteen years before he took his position on the throne. He went back to the shepherds' field. He faced challenges and struggles. He found himself hiding out in caves and running from his predecessor, King Saul, who saw that the "Lord was with David" and was jealous of the favor on David's life and wanted to kill him. There were several times when David could have killed King Saul and vindicated himself for all Saul did to him, but David walked in integrity. He resisted getting even because he knew who he was and he knew he carried an anointing. He was honoring God by protecting what God had placed on his life. David could have given up and wondered why he was facing so many challenges and he could have doubted the call of God on his life. However, he continued to remind himself that he was chosen and did not allow any of the difficulties to change his mind.

Now it's your turn. Do you believe you're chosen, or are you allowing people to talk you out of what God has called you to do? It is so important that you protect what is on your life. You carry a great anointing. Don't try to vindicate yourself and get even. Don't fight battles that aren't yours. Hold your head high and put your shoulders back. Scripture says you are a "royal priesthood" and "God's special possession." That means you are royalty. Adjust your crown and wear it like you know who you are.

My friend Jim is a successful man today with a beautiful wife and lovely children of his own. He would tell you that one of the greatest things he did for himself was to believe that he was chosen and valuable. He didn't let anyone disqualify him. He remembered his father's words that he was handpicked. In fact, Jim built such a strong foundation of belonging that when his sister would say to him, "Jim, Mom and Dad love you the most," he would reply, "Of course they do. They had to take you. I was chosen."

Receive this truth in your heart: You are chosen by God. He anointed you and put a calling on your life that is irrevocable. You are exceptional because He made you that way. He declares that His plans for you are for good, to prosper you and not to harm you. He has plans to give you a future and a hope.

God Has Packed Your Bags

I've been blessed to do a lot of traveling in my life. We have participated in over 195 Nights of Hope in arenas all over the country. No matter how many years I've been traveling, I still don't enjoy packing. You'd think I would have grown accustomed to it by now, but I still find myself looking in my bags the night before, thinking, *What have I left out? I don't want to get to where I am going and not have what I need.* Even today, every time I shut my suitcase, I say to myself, "I hope I haven't left anything out."

I think we can all feel that way at times, as if we

are missing something or that somehow we are lacking. We wonder if we are talented enough to land that job or receive that promotion. We question if we are smart enough to further our education, pretty enough to marry the man of our dreams, or funny enough for people to like us.

Can I tell you that God has packed your bags and He has left nothing out? You have everything you need to succeed in this life. God does not want us to doubt our worth and abilities. Don't go through life from a position of lack when God has made you more than enough. You have the qualities you need to have successful relationships, a good career, and a strong family. You have the right gifts, the right talents, and the right personality.

In the Bible, there is a man named Jeremiah who God had chosen to be a prophet to the Nations. Jeremiah felt unqualified and didn't know if he had the ability to speak to the people. He questioned God, asking, "How can I speak? I am only a child." Jeremiah didn't think he had what he needed. He felt empty and lacking. God did not leave him in his doubt and disbelief. The Lord told Jeremiah that he was equipped and He would go with him and tell him what to say. God was saying, "Jeremiah, I packed your bags. I chose you and completed you. You are lacking nothing."

I know it is easy to be like Jeremiah and doubt yourself. When I was a young teenager, my mother wanted me to work with her at my family's jewelry store on the weekends. I didn't feel like I knew enough about fine jewelry, and I was sure that I would embarrass myself and my mother if someone asked me a question and I didn't know the answer. But my mother lovingly encouraged me, even as I dragged my feet to the store each weekend. What I didn't realize was that my mother understood my fears and insecurities, but she also knew my gifts and talents. She knew I had everything inside me to succeed, but I had to move forward in faith one step at a time. She trained me through the years, and I began to learn more about the business and feel more confident. I wasn't lacking anything; I had within me the skills to be a good salesperson and spokesperson for the store. It was in that jewelry store that I met the man of my dreams. He came in for a watch battery and I sold him a brand-new watch. Over thirty years later, I am still crazy about him. It looks like Mother knows best after all.

My experience at the jewelry store taught me that God had already packed my bags, but it was up to me to unpack what He had put inside of me. I had the right gifts and talents for each assignment. It was up to me to push past my fears and insecurities. You too have the right gifts and talents. Your bags have been packed for your special assignments. The problem is too many of us are walking around with our bags packed but unopened. To unpack our bags, we have to push past fears, mistakes, and excuses in order to develop what God has placed in us.

Reaching new levels isn't always easy. Sometimes God will use people, new experiences, and even uncharted territory to nudge us out of our comfort zone. You may feel pressured today. Perhaps you feel some discomfort in your job or with your family. You may be facing a career change or an important decision about your future. Remind yourself that you have everything it takes. Reach deep inside of your bag and unpack what God has placed inside of you. Your faith may feel as if it's being tested and pushed to the extreme. Remember, it's the trial of your faith that brings out the lasting character in your life and builds confidence you cannot attain any other way.

The only difference between a piece of black coal and a precious diamond is the pressure it has endured. It is the pressure that it is under that turns that ordinary piece of coal into a rare and priceless jewel. The truth is the pressure you may be facing isn't going to break you—it's going to make you. It's going to develop you and give you experiences you need to build your confidence. Honor God and believe you have what it takes to shine brightly for Him.

Remember Your True Identity

How you see yourself will determine whether or not you reach your potential. God has created us in His image and crowned us with favor. But too often we allow our limitations and weaknesses, things that have happened to us, how we were treated, and mistakes we've made to distort that image. Rather than seeing ourselves as exceptional, full of potential, chosen by the Most High, we see ourselves as ordinary, thinking we've reached our limits. If my friend Jim would have seen himself as unwanted, if David would have seen himself as not qualified and left out, or if Jeremiah wouldn't have trusted that God would be with him, we wouldn't be talking about them. So take a moment to really consider: How do you see yourself? Have you taken on an image of yourself that is false, based on something that happened to you rather than the promises of God? We all face disappointments, we all make mistakes, but that's not who we are.

I'm here to remind you who you are. You are chosen; you are exceptional; you are handpicked by God. You weren't made to live defeated, depressed, addicted, and unfulfilled. You may have temporarily forgotten what being royalty means, but I believe things are changing, and you are remembering who you really are.

You are exceptional. You have everything you need. Unpack your bags, stir up your faith, and remember that you are royalty. Now, do your part and put your crown back on.

---◆---

EXCEPTIONAL YOU

I Declare

I am a chosen child of God, handpicked by Him and created in His image. I will not let my mistakes, my failures, or other people talk me out of who I am and Whose I am.

I am loved by God not because of my performance, not because I do everything perfectly, but because I am His child.

I am anointed and have the call of God upon my life to do great things.

I have everything I need to accomplish the dreams I have for my life—the

right gifts, the right talents, and
the right personality.

Because I am God's child, I am royalty, I
am His beloved, and I will walk each day
knowing my true identity.

Set Your Eyes on the Promises

How are you viewing your life today? Did you get up this morning ready to embrace the day? Or did you wake up weary, focused on the trials that you may be facing and the frustrations that lie in your path?

What we choose to focus on can make all the difference in our lives. To be exceptional means you are intentional with your attitude. You're looking for what's right in your life and being grateful for what you have. When we look for God's goodness and set our eyes on His promises, our thoughts will shift from defeat to victory.

Rearrange Your Thoughts

A few years ago, every time I walked into my living room, I'd think, *I don't like the way this room looks. I wish I could just get rid of all this furniture and start over. That would be so amazing.* As the days went by, any time I walked past that room, my attitude was sour. I would feel frustrated and I could hear myself complaining about it on the inside. Now, this was my living room. It was in the center of my house. I couldn't move that room. I couldn't avoid seeing it several times a day.

One day, when I realized that I probably wouldn't be getting new furniture anytime soon, I decided it was time to rearrange the furniture I did have. There was no one around to help me, so I put towels under the legs of the couch and began pulling the couch around, trying it in different locations. Then I moved a chair and a side table, and I even rearranged the lamps. When I finally finished, I stepped back, and to my delight, my perception of the room had changed completely. I stood there thinking: *I like this room. It looks really good.* I had a whole new attitude toward my furniture. I went and made myself a big glass of iced tea and sat on the couch to enjoy the view. I realized I had never seen that piece of furniture from that perspective. I thought, *It is so pretty. And look how the colors in that picture really pop next to those chairs.* I was able to have a fresh attitude toward my living room and see it differently because I rearranged it. Now when I walk past that room, I feel gratitude instead of frustration.

Sometimes we need to do the same thing to our thoughts. When you feel down and discouraged, you need to pay attention to what you are thinking. Just as I rearranged my furniture, we need to re-arrange our thinking so that we can see things from a new perspective. So often we don't pay attention to the way our thoughts affect our attitudes. Don't let your thoughts push you around; push your thoughts around and be made new in the attitude of your mind. Scripture says put on a fresh new attitude every day.

Have a Winning Attitude

You have heard the saying "Your attitude determines your altitude." It means that our attitudes have a direct correlation with the level of success in our lives. It means that while we can't always control our circumstances, we have the profound ability to control our attitude about our circumstances. When you take charge of your thoughts and attitudes, your life will go to new levels. Empower your life with positive thoughts of faith.

Joshua and Caleb provide a powerful example of how to ignite your faith with the right thoughts and attitudes. The Israelites had recently left Egypt under the leadership of Moses, where they had been living in bondage under Pharaoh. God delivered them with the promise of restoring Israel to the Land of Canaan, the Promised Land, which flowed with the abundance of provision. As they traveled to this new land, Moses sent twelve spies ahead of the tribe, including Joshua and Caleb, on an exploratory mission to scout out the Land of Canaan and find out as much as they could before the Israelites entered the land to take it as their own. He instructed them to bring back some of the fruit of the land for everyone to see.

The twelve spies were in Canaan for forty days and then returned to the Israelites with a huge cluster of grapes and amazing pomegranates and figs. Everyone marveled over the bounty, realizing the land was rich in produce and indeed flowing with abundance as they had heard. However, the rejoicing didn't last long, because ten of the spies began to talk about the problems they saw, spreading a bad report throughout the whole camp: "There are giants in the land. The cities have huge walls around them. We'll never be able to conquer those people. They are bigger than we are. In fact, we look like grasshoppers in our own sights, and so we are in their sight."

Joshua and Caleb, hearing the negative report, spoke up, saying, "If the Lord delights in us then He will bring us into the land and give it to us." They saw that the land was good. They also saw the fortified cities and how big the men were. However, they chose not to focus on the stature of the people;

they chose to focus on the size of their God. They saw how the Lord was with them, protecting and enabling them to go through the land for forty days unharmed. They remembered how God had parted the sea as they were leaving Egypt and drowned their enemies. They believed that if God had promised them this land, He would bring them into the land and give them the victory.

Ten spies chose to see themselves as grasshoppers whereas two spies saw their God as more than able to conquer.

A negative attitude can have devastating consequences. The report of the ten spies spread throughout the tribe. The Bible says the Israelites wept the whole night through. You would think they would remember the many miracles they had seen God perform, but they didn't. They took on the attitude of the negative report, thinking God had left them at the threshold of the Promised Land. They began to constantly grumble and complain, denying God's power in their lives. And because of their attitudes, they wandered in the wilderness for forty years, and no one over the age of twenty entered the Promised Land—with two exceptions.

Joshua and Caleb, whose faith never wavered, made it to the Promised Land. They had what the Bible referred to as "a different spirit." They chose to believe and obey, not according to what they saw, but according to what God said. While the rest of the adults died in the wilderness, Joshua and Caleb thrived because of their spirit of faith. After forty years, they were strong enough to lead the next generation into the land God had promised.

When you have the right attitude, you can look at your situation, no matter how challenging it may seem, and make it through by choosing to set your eyes on the promises of God. When you choose to see through your eyes of faith, not fear, you will come out of the wilderness moments stronger and more determined than you were before.

At eighty-five years old, Caleb declared, "I feel better than I ever have. I am as strong today as I was forty-five years ago, and I'm ready to take this land and destroy the giants" (see Josh. 14:10–12).

As they led the next generation into the Promised Land, Joshua's motto empowered them to understand the importance of a good attitude: "Choose you this day whom you will serve." He wanted them to know the choice was theirs. They didn't have to follow the crowd or the latest trends. They could choose what they wanted to focus on in life. As he encouraged them with his wisdom, he added: "As for me and my house, we're going to serve the Lord."

When you choose to serve the Lord, you quiet the discouraging voices that try to come against you by looking through your eyes of faith, not fear. You choose to believe that God is a Mighty God and He will do what He promised. He has already disarmed the power of the enemy. Don't focus on the giants, feeling overwhelmed by your circumstances, but rather focus on the promises of God that guarantee the victory. When we put on that winning attitude, it will shift the way we approach even the most challenging situations.

I have a friend who says she has a "lucky" shirt. And for every important business meeting, every presentation, every situation where she wants to feel confident that everything is going to go her way, she wears this shirt. Now, there is nothing special about that shirt. It isn't about the shirt, it is about the thoughts and attitude she has when she wears that shirt. She thinks, *Everything is going to go my way today. I'm going to succeed because I have my lucky shirt on.* But it's not the shirt that creates success. Her thoughts create a winning attitude. Her thoughts give her confidence that she has what it takes to succeed.

Every day you need to wake up believing that God has clothed you with His power. And that His goodness and mercy follow you all the days of your life. Then you will have the courage and boldness to move forward in faith as a victor and not a victim.

Lift Up Your Eyes

In the book of Genesis, Abraham was called by God to go on a journey of faith. What God promised Abraham looked impossible. Abraham moved forward in faith with his eyes on God. When God said,

"Leave your father's house," Abraham did as God instructed. He left the only home he knew with his family and his nephew Lot.

At the next stage of the journey, Lot and Abraham had to separate, because their possessions became so great that the land couldn't sustain both of them. Abraham was disappointed, but he trusted God. He told Lot to choose which direction he wanted to go. Lot looked at all the land and chose for himself a land that was flourishing with beauty and opportunity. When Abraham looked west, to where he was set to go, it didn't look like the lush land that Lot had chosen; it was much less desirable. It was at this point God spoke to Abraham and said, "Lift up your eyes and look from the place where you are. All the land that you can see, I will give it to you and your offspring forever" (see Gen. 13:14–15). Abraham had to lift his eyes from the disappointment and challenges of where he was and begin to look to the new things God wanted to show him.

It's interesting that the name *Lot* means "veil." When the two men parted ways, God lifted the veil from Abraham's eyes and he was able to see God in new ways. God wanted to reveal Himself to Abraham. As Abraham lifted his eyes, and as he looked beyond where he was, he began to see his destiny unfold. With lifted eyes he could look beyond where he was to the new places God was taking him.

In the same way, Scripture talks about how the veil has been lifted from our eyes. It has been torn in two by the power of Christ. Along your journey, God wants to show you things you haven't seen before. He wants to reveal Himself in powerful ways. He is saying the same thing to you that He said to Abraham, "Lift your eyes to Me, and I will show you the great things I am doing in your life."

It's easy to focus on what didn't work out, what didn't happen, the mistakes we've made, or what someone else did to us. Take your eyes off the problems that are trying to weigh you down and hold you back, and instead lift up your eyes and look at the promises of God. We can't set our eyes on the problems; we have to set our eyes on the promises. That's how we're going to rise above where we are right now. When we look for God, He always shows up.

A friend of mine was sitting in the waiting room

at a lawyer's office. She was feeling insecure and stressed out, trying to remember all the questions she had for the lawyer and praying that she would have the wisdom to remember and understand his answers. She felt overwhelmed and unsure in her abilities. She prayed, "God, how am I going to do this?" Reflecting back on a conversation we had, she remembered that when we feel overcome by a situation, we need to shift our eyes off the problem and look up to God. And so she did just that. She opened her eyes and looked up, and right above the door to her lawyer's office was a sign that read: PRAYER CHANGES EVERYTHING.

My friend had been to this office many times before and had never seen that sign. She knew it was a message from God, that He was by her side and she was not alone. With her head held high, she walked into that meeting with confidence and the assurance that God was with her. She asked all the questions she needed and understood the answers with total clarity.

God knows that there are times when we feel unsure or insecure, and overwhelmed by our circumstances. When we look to God in every situation, we must trust that He will show up and make a way for us to overcome our difficulties. God wants to build confidence in us so we can have faith that He will always be there for us.

How Big Is Your God?

Are you living with lifted eyes? Are you focused on how big the problem is or on how big our God is? Are you trusting God even when it doesn't make sense? He's directing your steps. He knows what you need. Keep walking in obedience and keep looking up.

This is what David did. He says, "I lift up my eyes to the mountains—where does my help come from? My help comes from the LORD, the Maker of heaven and earth" (Ps. 121:1–2). David knew that when he looked up at those mountains around Jerusalem, the blessings of God were there. That he had everything he needed—the provisions of God, the healing of God, the protection of God—because God had promised it.

God has amazing things in store for you, but you have to make a choice: "Am I going to look at my circumstances and get stuck, or am I going to believe that on the other side of my circumstances, God has greater things?" God is saying to you today, "Look up. I made you for more." Don't feel discouraged with where you are. This is not your final destination. Lift up your eyes and you'll see the greatness of our God. He always leads us to the Promised Land.

EXCEPTIONAL YOU

I Declare

My thoughts have incredible power. I will not allow negative thoughts to dictate my attitude and my day. I choose to push my thoughts around so I can see all the good that God has placed in my life.

I can't control my environment, but I can control my thoughts. I choose to serve the Lord and put on a winning attitude that shifts the way I approach even the most challenging situations.

I will not set my eyes on problems, on my circumstances, or whatever is trying to hold

me back. I will lift up my eyes and see the
greatness of my God.

I will set my focus on the promises of God.
No matter what giants I face, His promises
are greater.

I will have a different spirit, an excellent
spirit, and I believe that God is a big God.

Align Yourself with God

When I was a little girl, I loved to go to Galveston Beach with my family. We'd find a good spot, set up our blanket, and raise a red umbrella to shade us from the sun. As my parents sat down under the umbrella and grabbed cold drinks from the ice chest, I would run off to the water, where I would play for hours, getting lost in my thoughts and dancing in the waves.

Out from the shore, there are a series of sandbars that run parallel to the beach. One afternoon, I was feeling bold and left the first sandbar near the beach and swam through the deep part of the water until I reached the second sandbar. Even though I was pretty far from the shore, I was now standing in knee-deep water. I was quite proud of myself, having braved the deep water to get there, and I wanted my family to see me. I turned around, expecting to see my family under the familiar red umbrella, and while I could see lots of families, I couldn't find mine. I couldn't see that red umbrella.

I tried not to panic, but as a little girl, I knew I needed to find my family. I swam as quickly as I could back to shore. When I got there, I thought, *Which way do I go?* I headed to the left and walked and walked, scanning the crowd for my family, but I couldn't find them. So I turned back and retraced my steps, searching and searching for my family. Finally, in the distance, I saw that red umbrella. And can I tell you, as a little girl, that was a happy moment for me. I was finally calm and at peace, knowing where my family was and that I could make my way to them. I ran across the hot sand, flopped down under the umbrella, and decided that I was not going to do that again.

I hadn't meant to lose my way. I hadn't realized that, after playing in the water for a while, oblivious to everything around me, the current had caused me to slowly drift down the beach. The current was imperceptible to me. I was so busy playing in the water that I hadn't looked up to check in with my family or to stay in line with that red umbrella.

That's what happens in life sometimes. There are undercurrents in our life that can easily drag us off course from where we are supposed to be. Those undercurrents could be anger, bad attitudes, not forgiving others, or distractions, but they all have the same result—they lead us away from where God wants us to go.

I can't even count the number of times I've heard people say, "I was raised in church, so I don't know how I ended up so far away from God. I slowly drifted away from what I knew."

The other day, a woman was telling me how happy her marriage was in the early years, but then she and her husband began to argue. She said, "Now we've drifted apart and fight all the time. We don't see eye to eye. Things just aren't the same." Her distance from her husband was a result of the undercurrents that pulled her away from what was truly important.

Undercurrents can get us off course and separate

us from the important things God has placed in our lives. They can be so subtle that we don't even realize what's really happening. Those undercurrents can lead us away from the calling God has placed on our life, from our dreams, our goals, even from our family. We don't want to drift from those important things. But if we don't pay attention, that is exactly what happens. God wants us to notice those undercurrents and how they are affecting us so we can deal with them. He wants us to stay aligned with Him.

Fighting the Undercurrents

One of the best ways to keep from drifting from God's promises is to ask yourself tough questions about what is going on in your life. If you've just had a blowup with your spouse, maybe it's time to ask yourself, "Did I treat them with respect? Did I say something I shouldn't have? Am I honoring God with my choices?" Tough questions help realign and refocus us. We admit our mistakes, we ask for forgiveness, and then we get back on track. We have to be willing to evaluate our choices and make changes to our behavior if we want to stay on the best path. The undercurrents will always be there, but we can resist them if we're aware of which direction they are pulling us.

In Judges 13, an angel declared the coming birth of Samson, who was to become a man of great destiny. God gifted him with supernatural strength to deliver his people from the enemy, but Samson didn't take responsibility for what he had been given, and the undercurrents caused him to drift so far away from what he could have been. He let his guard down, set his eyes on the wrong things, began to rebel against what he knew was right, and as a result he was weakened in his morals.

If Samson had aligned himself with his purpose, he could have been everything God called him to be. If only he had checked his heart and asked God, "Am I on the right course? Am I walking humbly before You today? Am I using my gifts and talents to honor You?"

Samson could have dealt with the undercurrents in his life by not putting himself in compromising situations but rather by aligning himself with people who had the same values as he did. The Bible states, "Bad company corrupts good character" (1 Cor. 15:33). When you hang around the wrong people, you get yourself going in the wrong direction.

Hanging around the wrong people may not seem like a big deal. But if we don't take care of the small things, they'll become big things. Have you ever said something unkind just to let off some steam? Perhaps you're upset and throw around some harsh words to your family. You may think those are the small things, but they can cause damage to your family and can split relationships.

Undercurrents can be bad attitudes or laziness. These are the kinds of things that can cause us to lose good jobs. Sometimes we think temptations and distractions are just small things, but they cause us to drift. It's easy to start spending money that you don't have and getting yourself into financial difficulty. These are the small things. The Bible calls them "the little foxes that spoil the vines."

We live in a world that is full of undercurrents; we have to stay on guard. Maybe you've drifted and can identify some areas where you need to do better. It's never too late to get back in line with God. You can still become everything that He created you to be.

When you feel the undercurrents pulling you away from your set point, make the necessary adjustments that you need. Resist temptations and avoid distractions. God wants to help you overcome them. If Samson had done that, he would have avoided so much pain and wouldn't have ended up in the hands of his enemies, blinded and chained. If he had just asked for forgiveness and admitted his mistakes, saying, "Okay, I'm done with that. God, help me to be strong," he could have aligned himself with the victory God had planned for him.

You can start today. It's a new beginning. God's mercies are new every day. If you fall down, you don't have to stay down. You can get back up because of the mercy and the grace of Almighty God. Don't let one mistake fool you. Don't be like the person who eats a bowl of ice cream and then thinks, *Well, I already ate some, so let me just eat the whole gallon.* No, we can always realign. We can push away those temptations. God has given you power inside, but you have to set your mark and go for it.

The apostle Paul says, "Set your minds on things above, not on earthly things" (Col. 3:2). That means to set your mind on higher things, the valuable and important things in life—those things that are going to get you closer to your destiny, and cause you to have good families, strong relationships, and a great job. Sometimes we go through life not even thinking about what we're doing. We can't live on autopilot. God wants us to be intentional. We have to be on guard of what we are doing and what we are saying.

Hebrews 12 says to lay aside the weights and the sins that can easily entangle you. No matter how many mistakes you've made or where you find yourself today, it's never too late to get back in line with God. He has a purpose and a destiny for you. Now do your part, keep Him in your sight, and continue to strive toward the exceptional life God has for you.

God Is Doing a New Thing

We all go through times in our lives that can become all-consuming. Sometimes it can be a difficult situation, like a devastating diagnosis, or a family member's betrayal. It can be hard during those times to remember to ensure you're aligned with God. You have so many other things to think about. But it is exactly in those moments when we most need to look to God.

Many years ago, I faced a situation that left me feeling helpless, defeated, and unable to see the light. It was hard to find the hope and joy in each day. I was drifting, letting the undercurrent pull me away from who God called me to be. One day I felt like God was speaking to my heart and saying, "You cannot live like this. It is time for you to rise and shine. Lift your eyes and look beyond this problem at the new opportunities that I have in your future."

One of the names of God in the Old Testament is Jehovah Nissi. It means "the Lord our banner." One translation says, "The Lord our banner of victory and conquest." A banner is used to remember and commemorate; it identifies you as part of a certain group. Everywhere we go, God has put a banner of victory over our heads. It signifies this truth: "I am a child of the Most High God. I am destined to live in victory. I can do all things through Christ. When the enemy comes against me, I will raise my banner of victory."

I hadn't realized that I was allowing my feelings of defeat to stop me, block my blessings, and steal my purpose. I had to say, "No, I will not put on a cloak of defeat. I will raise my banner of victory." It wasn't easy. I didn't feel victorious every morning. But I continued to wave my banner of victory. I stayed aligned with God and His truth. I fought back against the undercurrents that wanted to lead me astray. I woke up each morning and proclaimed, "This problem cannot keep me from living in God's joy. I serve a great God, and He has amazing things in my future."

Knowing that God had placed this banner of victory over me, I was going to keep moving forward in the right direction so that God could continue to work in my life. This is what God spoke through the prophet Isaiah: "Forget the former things; do not dwell on the past. See, I am doing a new thing! Now it springs up; do you not perceive it? I am making a

way in the wilderness and streams in the wasteland"
(Isa. 43:18–19).

Sometimes we can focus in on the wasteland and
forget that God is forging new streams. We begin to
think that God can work only when we get out of
the wilderness. But no, God can work even then. We
don't have to wait for our difficult situations to be
resolved before God will do a new thing. He is always
at work in our lives. When we learn to look up from
our problems and the challenges that we face, and
keep our eyes on God and how He is making a way,
we can move forward in faith and begin to live the
exceptional life God has planned for us.

It was during those years, when the situation
wasn't resolved, that God showed me amazing things
and uncovered gifts and talents in myself that I
didn't know I possessed. Ultimately, God vindicated
me and resolved the situation that had caused so
much stress. By the end of it all, I was stronger than
before and more steeped in God's promises. God
wasn't waiting for that situation to be resolved to do
new things. He was at work even in the midst of my

difficulties. If I would have stayed in defeat, I would have missed out on the God-given opportunities He had in store for me during that time.

God doesn't want us to stop living when things get tough, but to keep looking for where He is leading us. Don't focus on an area of your life that needs to change or on something that's not happening. Don't wait for God to answer all your prayers before you can move forward. God has new things springing up even now.

He didn't say that you would never go through the wilderness or the wasteland. He didn't say you'd never wonder, *Why did this happen to me?* But God did say, "You're not going to stay where you are. I can make a way in the wilderness." He can refresh you during the times you feel weary, and He can do the impossible as long as you look up to see it and stay aligned with Him. Don't get so focused on the stresses of life that they blur your vision. Look up from where you are and take in all the life that God has given you. There is more in store beyond where you are right now.

EXCEPTIONAL YOU

I Declare

I will not allow the undercurrents of life to lead me away from the calling God has placed on my life, from my dreams, from my goals, from my family.

I will evaluate my choices and when necessary make changes to my behavior to stay in line with God. I will not put myself in compromising situations or align myself with people who do not share my values.

I will stay on my guard, resist temptations, and avoid distractions.

I will set my mind on "things above"—the valuable and important things that are going to get me closer to my destiny, that cause me to have a good family, strong relationships, and a great job.

I may be in a difficult time, but God is doing a new thing; even today it is springing up. I will learn to perceive the ways that He is at work in my life.

Encourage Yourself

The other day, I received an email from a young woman who told me about a hardship she'd recently faced. She'd thought she and her boyfriend were heading in the direction of marriage, but one day he told her that he was moving out of state to take a new job. This news shocked her. She couldn't believe that he could decide to leave without even discussing it with her. She realized that he didn't love her the way she'd thought he did and that their relationship was not as special to him as it had been to her.

The first few weeks after the breakup, she said, "I tried and tried to make sense of what happened. What did I do wrong? I blamed myself because things didn't work out. I was consumed with these negative thoughts. I became so discouraged that I didn't want to go to work or out with friends. I just wanted to stay home. One evening, I was flipping through the channels and came across your television program. As I began to listen to the message that Joel gave that day, it was as if he was talking to me. I immediately felt encouraged. I began to listen to the messages on your podcast and on YouTube every chance I had. As I heard those words of encouragement, hope rose within me. I became stronger and regained my confidence. I realized I had been so focused on what happened to me that I wasn't paying attention to what was happening inside me. I was allowing what someone had done to me to define my future. I had been feeling so hurt, so discounted, and so alone, that it was causing me to throw away all the good things in my life. I realized whether that man chose to love me or not, I was still the same. My purpose and value hadn't changed. I started to put into practice the teaching I heard in your ministry. I began to look in the mirror every day and say to myself, 'You are beautiful. You are talented. You are valuable.' As I practiced this, it became easier and easier to believe. I started to appreciate myself and began to like who I saw in the mirror; the fun person I really am and always have been."

Then she closed her email with this: "Every day I say to myself, 'God is going to bring the right person across my path because I'm in the palms of His hands.'"

That young woman made a choice to overcome the discouragement she had been feeling by speaking words of faith to herself. She used her words to build herself up and rewrite the negative narrative in her mind with the truth of who God says she is. As she began to encourage herself, hope rose in her heart, hope that produced faith, which helped her move forward into her future. Disappointments, hurts, and unfair situations will come to all of us, but we can't allow memories of those situations to dominate our lives. To be exceptional, you must pay attention to what your thoughts are creating inside you. Your thoughts are powerful. They can lift you up or push you down. Your thoughts can create an atmosphere of victory or defeat. This woman chose the right thoughts and spoke the right words over her life, and as a result, she went from a victim mentality to a victor mentality.

In Exodus 6, Moses told the Israelites that God was going to deliver them from the hard labor and oppression they were facing under Pharaoh in the land of Egypt. He was reporting to them that God was going to bring them out of bondage into a place of freedom. Because they were so broken and despondent, they didn't listen to what Moses was saying to them. Scripture says that they were too discouraged to believe. Discouragement can drown out the promises of God. Discouragement can dash our hopes and dreams and keep us from believing that we have a bright future. It can bury our faith and weigh us down. Things don't always turn out the way we would like. Difficulties are a part of life; however, it is up to us to learn how to encourage ourselves with the promises of God. The woman who was shattered from her broken relationship would tell you that although her relationship with that man was not restored, God did restore her faith and joy, and she was able to move forward with her life.

Fill Your Tank of Encouragement

David was a great king, a man after God's own heart, who learned the importance of encouraging himself in the Lord. This mighty man of God, who faced great challenges, knew the secret to overcoming. He built himself up by filling his mind with the things of God. He was able to draw strength when he needed it from what was inside him. David had just suffered the worst defeat of his life, and the men in his army were so disheartened that they threatened to stone him. At his lowest point of discouragement, when he had no one around him to encourage him, David "encouraged and strengthened himself in the Lord his God" (1 Sam. 30:6 AMPC).

It's great when your family and friends are there to encourage you during difficult times, but what happens when no one's there to encourage you? We shouldn't depend on other people to encourage us. Our main source of encouragement should come from within. You can't look to other people to find your encouragement; you have to encourage yourself. I can't even imagine Joel trying to encourage me every time I feel discouraged. If I went to him each time I felt pressured and needed to be cheered up, he'd probably lock himself in a closet and not come out. And I wouldn't blame him. We can't depend on other people to keep us happy.

David believed that he was chosen and that he was called by God to do great things. He gave praise to God in his difficulties and filled up his emotional tank by getting into agreement with God. Too often we get out of agreement with God when we make a mistake or when things don't go our way. We are critical about ourselves and we talk negatively about our situations. We find it easy to recognize the good qualities in other people, yet completely ignore our own positive qualities. Instead, we seem to only see what we're doing wrong, or all the times we blow it. We have to remind ourselves that we are not failures; we are learners.

If you're going to be exceptional, you must learn to encourage yourself. Get up every day and begin to declare who God says you are. "I am a child of the

Most High God. I am loved by God. I am strengthened by God. I am accepted by God, and I am full of purpose and destiny." This will change the atmosphere of your life, and then you will have treasure stored up in your heart to draw from. As you continue to encourage yourself, you will have the ability to see the best not only in yourself, but also in others.

Your Words Have Power

In the beginning, Scripture says that God *spoke* to the darkness and created light. Then He began to use His *words* to create the world. Words have creative power. Scripture says there is life and death in the power of the tongue. We have the ability to speak life to those we love and help them discover what God has placed inside them. Words can lift us up or push us down. What you say matters and has a profound impact on all those around you.

In the book of James, the writer compares the tongue to the rudder of a big ship. The rudder may be a very small part, but it controls the entire direction of the ship. How the pilot directs the rudder determines where the ship will go. Even with strong winds and raging waters, that small rudder has the power to turn the ship. But who controls the rudder? The pilot.

Maybe you're in a storm today; the winds are raging against you. You will be tempted to complain, blame others, or speak doubt into the situation. Negative words will not steer you out of the storm. I encourage you to pilot your ship with the rudder of faith-filled words. When you resist the temptation to speak negative words, you will direct your life out of the rough waters and set your course for victory.

David prayed, "Set a guard over my mouth, LORD; keep watch over the door of my lips" (Ps. 141:3). Even as David used his words to encourage himself, he was also mindful of his choice of words. David was in a very difficult situation. He was stuck in a cave with enemies all around him. David was saying, "Lord, don't let me send my life in the wrong direction. Keep my tongue from speaking evil." He knew the power of his words.

The pressures of life are real. It's easy to speak

out of frustration. We too need to keep a guard over our mouths in times of stress and pressure. We all face difficult times that weigh heavy on us. When I don't know what to say, I just begin to praise God and thank Him. I say, "Father, thank You that You are stronger than anything that is coming against me. God, it may look bad, but You are good. You can do anything but fail me." Then I begin to sing the worship songs that we sing every week in church. I have those songs in my heart so they come out of my mouth. I praise my way to victory. God has given us the ability to use our words and release our faith so we can pilot our lives through the storms and straight to Jesus.

Go After Your Miracle

Mark 5 tells the story about the woman who had suffered with bleeding in her body for twelve long years. She had been to many doctors and had done everything she could. She spent all of her money trying to find a cure, but she wasn't getting better, only worse. She was frail and weak. One day she found out Jesus was passing through her town, so she went to see Him. I am sure she had heard stories of how He had healed a crippled man, cured another from leprosy, and made blind men see. Something came alive inside her and she thought, *If He did this for other people, He could certainly do this for me.* The streets were crowded and buzzing with people. She could have been thinking, *I'll never be able to make it through all the people in the streets. I am weak and exhausted.* She could have been complaining, saying, "Life isn't fair. Why did this happen to me?" Instead she said to herself, "If I can only get to Jesus and touch the hem of His garment, I know I will be healed." One version says, "She *kept* saying to herself. She repeated it over and over, 'When I get to Jesus, I know I will be well. I know healing is coming. I may be weak and exhausted, but my miracle is on the way.' " It was the words of faith coming out of her mouth that gave her the strength to go after her miracle. She encouraged herself along the way so she could keep going.

The streets were crowded with people, and her body was weak and frail because she had been losing blood for years. Instead of looking at the problem, she began to release faith-filled words that gave her the ability and strength that day to get out of her home and begin to push through the crowd. Most people would have given up, but not this woman. She was determined and had a made-up mind. She found herself in the crowd near Jesus. I can see her now, pushing through and saying to herself, "If I can only get to Him, if I can touch Him." She came up behind Jesus and gave one last, "If I can only get to Him." With her final bit of strength and determination, she stretched out her hand and touched the hem of His robe. Immediately she knew her life was changed.

Jesus turned around, looked at that woman, and saw her faith. He said, "Woman, you are healed."

Her words led her to her miracle and changed the course of her life. In order to get her miracle, she not only had to fight through the crowd of people that day, she had to fight through the thoughts that could have crowded her mind.

Is your mind crowded with thoughts that are telling you, *You will never meet the right person* or *You will never see your dreams come to pass*? The crowd could be negative words people have spoken over you. *You're not good enough. You don't have the talent you need. You will never be successful.* You may have to fight through the crowd of broken dreams, financial problems, or mistakes you made. The crowd could be telling you to stay home. You have tried everything and it is not going to work out. If you are going to be exceptional, you have to be more determined than the crowd of thoughts that are coming against you.

Jesus is passing by. Expect things to change. Keep encouraging yourself: "My breakthrough is coming. Opportunities are on the way."

Jesus said, "My words are spirit and they are life."

I want to encourage you to take the words of God and speak them audibly out of your mouth. It will change your thoughts and lead you to your miracle.

When that woman said, "If I can only touch Him, I'll be healed," she prophesied her future. The winds or storms may be coming against you, but you can direct your ship with the words you speak. You can pass through those storms and get on the course to your miracle today. Your words can lead you to the very garment of Jesus.

EXCEPTIONAL YOU

I Declare

I am responsible to encourage and strengthen myself in the Lord my God and His promises. I cannot depend on my family or friends to encourage me.

I will fill my encouragement tank by getting in agreement with what God says about me. I am fearfully and wonderfully made in the image of God.

My thoughts have the power of encouragement. Today, I am going to choose thoughts of victory and treasure them up in my heart, so I can draw strength from them in times of discouragement.

Words have creative power. I will set a guard
over my mouth and be careful to speak
words of faith that set my life on a course of
victory. I will not speak negative words.

Travel Light

Joel and I do a lot of traveling these days, and a few years ago we had two work-related trips that were scheduled back-to-back. When we arrived home from the first trip, we were only going to be there for about two hours before we had to turn around and head back to the airport. The entire plane ride home, all I could think about was getting my dirty clothes out of my suitcase. Thinking about that week's worth of laundry in my bags, I couldn't face the idea that we were going on another trip that night. As soon as I arrived home, I dumped all those dirty clothes into the hamper and began to put clean clothes in my suitcase. It was the craziest thing, but even though I was tired and anxious on the trip home, as soon as

I refreshed my bags with clean clothes, I took on a whole new attitude. I was energized and ready to go on the next trip.

It is the same way in life—if our bags are cluttered with old hurts, regrets, and unforgiveness, we can't look forward to the next thing God is bringing about because we're still bogged down with dirty laundry. Some people never refresh their bags. Their bags are stuffed with who offended them, how they were mistreated, and what didn't work out. All that dirty laundry weighs them down and makes them feel tired and discouraged.

We all have a decision to make as to what we carry with us into each day. What we pack in our bags is either an investment into where we're going or where we have been. Investing in our past means we focus on what didn't work out, on who hurt us, or the mistakes we made. If we are not careful, we find ourselves repeating the refrain of *if only*: "If only I had been raised in a better environment. If only I had finished college, I could get a better job. If only I had spent more time with my kids, I wouldn't be dealing with this."

Those thoughts are a waste of time and energy and a bad investment in our future. You can't do anything about what happened in the past, but you can do something about right now. When you begin to focus on what you can change instead of what you can't change, you are making the right investment. The past is the past. God didn't create you to carry around a bunch of junk that is going to weigh you down and keep you from the life He has planned for you.

Every day we need to refresh our bags. When you wake up in the morning, clear out the clutter and those things that didn't work out the day before. Forgive the people who hurt you. Forgive your spouse for what they said. Let your children off the hook for not noticing all you do for them. Forgive yourself for the mistakes you made. Let go of the setbacks and disappointments of yesterday and start fresh and new. Where you're going is much more important than where you've been. If you're going to be exceptional, you have to travel light.

I knew a woman who had been divorced for a couple of years, and she had been praying fervently that God would bring someone into her life. She eventually met a man she was very excited about. He was kind, successful, had a great job, and loved God. She was so thrilled about the possibilities, but instead of starting fresh, she made the mistake of constantly talking about what she had been through in her first marriage and how her husband had mistreated her. She was carrying around all of her negative baggage from the past into this new relationship. After a while the man told one of her friends that she was so focused on her past and what she had been through that it impeded their ability to make a good connection. He decided to move on and ended their relationship.

That's what happens when you don't refresh your emotional bags—you carry your stinky stuff everywhere you go. You can't drag around negative baggage from the past and expect to have a bright future. No matter what somebody did or how unfair it was, let it go. Don't let it continue to pollute your life.

The apostle Paul said, "One thing I do, forgetting those things which are behind and reaching forward to those things which are ahead" (Phil. 3:13 NKJV).

He was saying, "I don't look back at my past mistakes and relive my failures. I don't look back at the people who wronged me or the situations that didn't work out. I don't dwell on the disappointments, the hurts, and the bad breaks. I forget what's behind and I get ready for the new things God wants to do." He understood that you can't go forward while looking backward.

Joel and I used to play racquetball together. It's a fast game that's played with a hollow rubber ball and racquet in a fully enclosed court. The one safety rule to this game is that you never look back because the ball comes off the back wall so fast that it can hit you in the face and cause significant injury. No matter where you are on the court, you have to keep facing forward and play the ball in front of you.

Life is a lot like racquetball. Looking back at your past mistakes and reliving your failures will only cause damage. Dwelling on past hurts and who did you wrong will ruin your relationships, lower your self-esteem, and steal your confidence. To live in the "I wish I had done it different" or "Why did this happen?" will limit your potential and rob you of your passion. You cannot undo your past, but you can do something about your present. You can play the ball that is in front of you, not the ball that's behind you. Do what the apostle Paul did: "Don't look back." God will take what the enemy meant for harm and use it to your advantage. Reach forward to those things that are ahead of you and take your swing. That's where your success lies.

Shut the Door to the Past

A few years ago, Joel and I were invited to a highly secured government building. To enter the building, we had to go through two sets of double doors about fifteen feet apart. We stood in front of the first set of doors, they opened, and we walked through them to the second set of doors. However, the second set would not open until the first set closed.

As long as you continue to talk about the wrongs that happened to you, reliving the mistakes and failures and feeling sorry for yourself, you are keeping those doors open. When we hold on to our past, the new set of doors won't open. It's time to let the doors of disappointment close behind you so you can step forward into the new things God has in store.

I once met a man who told me how difficult his life had been growing up. He witnessed his brother's life ending in a tragedy and told me about how his girlfriend had died in the prime of her life. He said, "As a young man, I faced so many negative things and became so bitter that I had suicidal tendencies. I felt as though I couldn't live with what had happened to me. I couldn't get past the past. I couldn't move forward.

"One day," he continued, as the expression on his face brightened, "I woke up and for some reason I began to cry out to God, saying, 'God, help me move past all this bitterness. Help me take hold of what You have in store for me.'"

He had a strong urge to start running. He didn't understand why, but he put on his tennis shoes and went out and began to run. "Every day as I would run," he recalled, "I would imagine myself shutting the door to the dark past and running toward my bright future. With every run, I felt God in front of me, helping me and urging me forward." As the man continued to run, God began to change his heart and refresh his mind. That's how he practiced closing the door to his past. He said, "As I kept running every day, running farther than I ever had before, I saw how God was coming alongside me, helping me accomplish things I had never thought possible." This attitude spread throughout his life. He went back and finished college; then he enrolled in medical school. Today, he has a successful medical practice with thirty-five employees and his own clinic.

Just as this man was able to overcome his challenges because he called out to God, you too can press past anything that's trying to hold you captive. Whether it's anger, bitterness, or regret, find your way to close the door to the past. God will help you. Maybe you need to quit talking about your past or stop associating with the people who keep bringing it up. God is saying it's time to move forward into the new things He has in store. Nothing that happened in your past has to keep you from the amazing future in front of you. You can make the decision to shut the door to the hurts, disappointments, and mistakes. It's time to move forward into what God has in store.

Scripture says to renew your mind with God's Word and transform your thinking. When you hear those negative voices telling you that you can't rise any higher and it's never going to get any better, be quick to say, "No, thanks, that's not for me. I am going to stockpile good thoughts." Make a decision that you are going to become everything God intended you to be. You may have been hurt, but you are well on your way to recovery.

Every Sunday during the prayer time at our church, Joel makes declarations of faith over our congregation. He declares, "You are blessed. You are focused. You are disciplined, talented, and well able to do what God has called you to do." He makes those declarations of faith over us each week. What he is doing is putting into our thinking what God says about us and reminding us who we are and what we are able to do. God's Word works when you put it into your heart and mind. Every day you should make declarations of faith over your own life. Declare over yourself that you are healed, you are blessed, and you are more than a conqueror. God is the healer of all things, and if you will remember the good and step out in faith, He will take you to the place of complete healing so you can live the life of victory.

Release the Weight of Worry

This is what worry does to us. It weighs us down and prevents us from enjoying our life. Scripture says that worry cannot add an inch to your height or a single hour to your life (see Matt. 6:27). Have you ever considered all the things you worried over that never came to pass? Someone once said: "I've been through some terrible things in my life, some of which actually happened."

God doesn't want us to live that way. To become exceptional, you have to travel light. Put aside the worries and walk forward into each day expecting miracles, finding joy, and believing in God's provision.

I've been married to Joel for over thirty years, and

every morning he makes the declaration, "Today is going to be a great day." It's so important that we set the tone for the day. We all have lists of things to accomplish and tasks that need to be attended to, and every one of those things can bring stress. But we can't let those lists steal us away from what is truly important. We have to resist the temptation to start off worried, thinking about what's wrong and all the difficulties. Start the day in faith, casting your worries on the Lord, trusting that He's guiding and directing your steps.

There is a story in Scripture about two sisters who welcomed Jesus into their home. When they heard He and His disciples were on their way, they must have been extremely excited. But there was cleaning to be done and food to prepare. Jesus was a guest of great honor, and they wanted Him to be comfortable.

Once Jesus arrived, one sister, Martha, was pulled away to the kitchen, focused on all the preparations that still needed to be made to feed Jesus and His disciples. She was running around frantically trying to make everything perfect. She was so busy that she forgot to stop and enjoy the company that was in her home that day. Her sister, Mary, however, sat at Jesus' feet. She wasn't going to miss this opportunity to be in His presence. After a while, Martha became frustrated and said, "Lord, don't you care that my sister has left me to do the work by myself? Tell her to help me."

Jesus said to her, "Martha, Martha, why are you so anxious and troubled about so many things?" He not only called her name once, He called it twice. He knew she was so caught up in her to-do list that she was missing the moment in front of her. He wasn't disregarding the things that needed to be done. He was addressing how she was handling her responsibilities.

He said, "Martha, only one thing is needed. Mary has chosen what is better, and it will not be taken away from her." He was saying, "All the concerns, the crises, the things that are causing you stress, bring to My feet. Stay in My presence, allow Me to fill you." That's the better way to handle worry and stress.

It takes the same amount of energy to worry as it does to believe. Don't let your mind dwell on the negative. You may have a good reason to worry, but worry is not only strangling your joy and peace, it limits what God will do. When you believe, angels go to work; when you believe, negative situations will turn around; when you believe, dreams come to pass.

Paul said in Philippians 4, "Do not be anxious about anything, but in everything by prayer and supplication, giving thanks to God, let your request be made known" (see v. 6). God knows that there will be times we feel overwhelmed. Paul didn't just say, "Don't be anxious." He told us how to win the war on worry. He said, "Pray about everything." Instead of worrying, pray, ask God to help you. Take your worry list and make it your prayer list. Talk to God about everything that concerns you. That's what prayer is. He wants to help us through life, but He's waiting for us to come to Him. Don't be like Martha, so busy and stressed. Slow down and invite Him into your situation. Thank Him that He's working, thank Him that He's fighting your battles, thank Him that He's bigger than what you're facing. When you welcome Him into the middle of your challenges, you'll have strength that you didn't have, peace when you could be upset, and faith to enjoy each moment.

Live this day in faith, trusting that God's in control. He knows what you need. Scripture says that a sparrow doesn't fall to the ground without our Heavenly Father knowing about it (see Matt. 10:29). How much more does He care about you? Cast those worries that are weighing you down on Him. Shift your perspective and stop carrying the problems that might never come. Get up each morning and make the declaration, "Today is going to be a good day." When you put this into practice, you'll live the exceptional life that belongs to you.

I Declare

I will not look back and obsess over what didn't work out, on who hurt me, or the mistakes I made. I will let the past be the past and fix my gaze forward to what God has in store.

I can't do anything about what happened in the past, but I can do something about right now. I will begin to focus on what I can change instead of what I can't change.

Every morning I will clear out the clutter and the things that didn't work out the day before and start fresh and new.

I won't allow a painful experience to trick me into thinking I am going to have a painful life. God is the healer of all hurts. I will renew my mind with God's Word and transform my thinking.

I will bring all the things that are causing me stress to Jesus and leave them with Him. In His presence I will receive the fullness of peace and joy. I will turn my worry into worship.

Love Well

My mother is one of the most encouraging people I know. I saw her sincerely encourage people every day as I grew up. Through her example, she taught my brother and me to not only look for the best in people, but also to make deposits of encouragement into their lives. She always told me, "Victoria, there is something special about every person you meet. You just need to take the time to look for it and tell them."

The something special didn't need to be huge. It could be a sparkle in someone's eyes, or the brightness in their smile, or a job well done on a simple task. A simple compliment can hold great power for someone. It can help them get through the day. Make it a habit to find that one good thing in the people in your life.

Spread your words of encouragement widely. Your words can literally put someone back on their feet. Your words hold the power to keep them strong and give them confidence.

Scripture says to encourage one another daily, as long as it's called today. Have you encouraged someone today? When God says to encourage one another daily, there is an exchange that takes place. Not only will you give encouragement but also that encouragement will come back to you. When we become encouragers, we cause others to rise higher and our lives go to new levels too. We hold the power to lift one another up, every day, to remind one another of the goodness of God. Let's not hold back those life-giving words, but rather look for ways to bring the love of God into the lives of others.

Rise Up

Years before Joel's father died and he became pastor of the church, I would often tell Joel that he was a disciplined and smart person. I would find ways to compliment his dedication and commitment. Sometimes I felt the Lord give me particular Scriptures for Joel when I was reading my Bible. They would seem to jump off the page and I knew they were something that Joel needed to hear. I would write them down and place them in spots where I knew he would find them. He would always thank me and tell me that my assurance and support gave him tremendous confidence and perseverance, but what I didn't realize was the impact that encouragement would have on my own life. Joel tells me to this day that one of the reasons he felt like he could step up and take over when his father passed away was because of all that time I encouraged him and the times I told him what he could do and what he was becoming.

When he stepped up, our family stepped up. When he moved forward, our whole family moved forward. When the water in the harbor rises, all the ships rise. Don't withhold encouragement, because it will always come back to you. The Bible says, "A generous person will prosper; whoever refreshes others will be refreshed" (Prov. 11:25). When we speak encouragement to others, we not only breathe God's love into them, but we also breathe God's love into our own soul.

One of the greatest places we can begin to practice this simple truth is in our own home. Tell the people in your life how much they mean to you. Change the atmosphere in your home by encouraging your spouse and your children. It's easy to point out what's wrong. Instead, let's begin to point out what is right, and what the other person does well. Bring value into the lives of those around you by catching them doing things right. Anyone can see what's wrong. People will not always live up to our expectations. We all have shortcomings. Let's be people who are willing to catch people doing what is right.

The other day, I ran into a friend of mine whom I've known for several years. She is a sharp, talented woman who has a strong personality and can be quite opinionated. She was telling me about a recent argument she'd had with her husband. She ended the story with how she set him straight.

As I looked at the smile on her face that seemed to imply she felt a sense of accomplishment, I asked a simple question: "Do you think your husband is a loser?"

She looked at me in shock and immediately said, "No." She went on to explain how he was incredibly successful and was about to be promoted again.

I nodded and said, "Who wins most of the disagreements at home?"

"Me," she said quickly. She had gotten into the habit of pointing out all her husband did wrong; she was making her husband the loser. Quite simply, he was a winner at work, but at home he was always a loser. We want to help our loved ones feel like winners, because that is what they are. We are called to encourage them, cheer them on, and build them up.

We need to be looking for ways that we can be cheerleaders in the lives of our loved ones. Think about cheerleaders on the sidelines of a football game. They don't put down their pom-poms when the other team scores. They don't walk off the field when the team makes mistakes; they cheer harder. They know that their words of encouragement can push the team past their mistakes and on toward a winning goal.

We are called to be encouragers and to love one another well. This is how we bring about God's blessing in our lives.

You Have a Superpower

You can literally defeat the power of the enemy in the life of someone by your encouragement. The enemy wants to bring feelings of discouragement. He wants to take courage away and subtract from what God is doing. When we encourage one another, our encouragement is a weapon that can defeat the schemes of the enemy. We become like action heroes when we understand the power that encouragement holds. Your positive words and actions can bring healing and wholeness to someone else. Scripture says to encourage one another daily...so that none of you may be hardened in your hearts by sin's deceitfulness. Encouragement can bring light into dark situations and refresh our spirits when we feel tempted to give in to despair.

In Houston, we've had countless floods over the last few years that have been devastating to our community. Many of the staff in the church have had to abandon their homes quickly without warning. They had to leave so fast that they couldn't even take the time to bring anything with them. The floodwaters came swooping in and it was a matter of life or death to get on those rescue boats.

One of our staff members told me about how discouraged she was as they sat in the shelter. She was grateful for their safety but fearful their house was being destroyed along with all of their earthly possessions left her feeling defeated and empty inside.

Several days later they were finally able to get back into their house; it made everything even worse to see that her fears had come true. There was so much damage that they would have to start over. As they picked through the debris, sodden clothing, and destruction, her husband said, "We have to change our focus and go up to the church to begin to help distribute supplies and help other people." He was trying his best to get the attention off their loss and become a blessing to someone else.

But his wife couldn't even imagine leaving to help others. She said, "I can't. I don't have clean clothes or any makeup or even a hairbrush to pull my hair back. I can't even shower to feel clean." She kept falling deeper and deeper into despair. Nothing was normal; she couldn't believe all that had been taken from her, and she wasn't sure how she was going to make it through this crisis in her life.

And then she heard a familiar voice. She looked up to see some friends whose houses had been spared from the floodwaters. They had come over to see what they could do to help. But they hadn't come empty-handed. Her friend held in her hand a bag of makeup. She had pulled together all the essentials, in just the right shades, to help her friend start to feel like herself again.

That act of encouragement was what this woman needed to take the next step. It's what she needed to move forward and out of this place of despair. That simple act of putting on makeup and pulling back her hair imparted courage and perspective. She said to her husband, "Honey, I guess now I'm ready to go down to the church and help someone else."

Her friend showed up that day as an action hero in her defense. Her friend couldn't change the fact that five feet of water flooded her home, but she could become a part of the healing and restoration in the life of her friend. She imparted courage and bravery into that woman. Sometimes encouragement is as simple as showing up with a mop or a broom or a bag of makeup. Those small acts can make a powerful impact. That is what it means to love well.

Ecclesiastes says it this way: "Two people are better off than one, for they can help each other succeed. If one person falls, the other can reach out and help" (Eccles. 4:9–10 NLT). God isn't just talking about a marriage relationship; He's talking about reaching out to those around you. That is the healthy way to live. That is the way God designed it. God has ordained people in your life for you to strengthen as well as people to strengthen you. None of us have gotten where we are by ourselves. We have all been helped, supported, and encouraged along the way.

We are better together. God designed us to be in community. There are times when we feel like it is easier to do things on our own and we don't need any help. People can be difficult and challenging at times. But you won't reach your highest potential by yourself. You've seen how birds fly in formation. They do that because it makes the trip easier. They use 40 percent less energy when they fly together.

They could fly by themselves but they understand they go farther with fewer struggles when they are together.

Over thirty times in Scripture we find the phrase *one another*. Love one another. Encourage one another. Serve one another. Comfort one another. You need "one another" around you. Don't isolate yourself and think, *Well, I'm strong enough. I'm tough enough. I'm talented enough to be on my own.* You may be for what *you* have in mind but not for what *God* has in mind. He has something bigger, something more rewarding that you can't do by yourself. Are you flying solo? Or do you have a community of faith? People flying with you, watching over you, encouraging you, inspiring you?

You have something to offer that no one else can give. Someone needs your encouragement. Someone needs to know that you believe in them and you believe that they can succeed. We can't just obsess over how we can make our lives better, how we can get ahead and succeed. We should always be willing to take time to make someone else's life better. Our attitude should be: *Who can I encourage today? Who can I build up?*

If you are feeling down today, if you are feeling discouraged, encourage someone else. Push someone else forward. I believe this is the principle of sowing and reaping in action. When you step out to help someone else, you are really helping yourself—you are sowing seeds for happiness in your future.

Strengthen Your Roots

The enemy wants to bring division and discord into your relationships. He will work overtime to keep you upset about what someone said or what they did. The apostle Paul says, "Make every effort to keep the unity of the Spirit through the bond of peace" (Eph. 4:3). He is saying we have to *choose* to keep unity. Look for ways you can draw people closer and love them well. The Bible says blessed are the peacemakers. *Peacemakers* is a compound word. Peace doesn't just come. You have to make peace. Making peace means looking for the ways that you can encourage and bind people together. It's not easy or simple to be in relationships. It takes effort and determination, but it's worth it.

We were made to live together, and when we live in unity with the supportive community that God has graced us with, we have a stronger foundation to face the diagnoses and the tragedies, to withstand the storms of life, with more strength because we are not facing them alone.

Did you know that the giant redwood trees in Northern California that grow 350 feet tall and 22 feet wide at the base are supported by roots that descend only 5 to 6 feet into the ground? Now, it seems impossible, given how tall they are, that their roots do not go deeper. But instead of growing deep in the ground, the roots of the redwood trees spread wide. They extend sometimes up to 100 feet out from the tree. They have a broad base of support, not just because of how wide the roots travel but because they grow in groups of trees called *groves*. The roots of these trees intertwine and even fuse with the roots of the other trees. This network of support gives them tremendous strength to withstand high winds and raging floods. Because their roots intertwine, they share nutrition, one tree helping to feed the next, which helps them survive in periods of drought.

God has designed us to be in community, to love one another, encourage one another, and help one another rise above the difficulties that come our way. If we could be as united in our lives as those redwood trees are, I believe we could withstand any of life's storms and droughts. Who are you intertwined with today? Don't destroy your roots. Keep them strong and nourished, so that you may live in unity, in peace, and with the strength and blessings of God. Be an encourager each and every day and watch your community grow strong, tall, and able to withstand any attack from the enemy.

Be on the Lookout

Everywhere we go, we should be on the lookout for ways we can be a blessing. God puts people in our path. He gives us opportunities to be good to them.

It doesn't have to be something big that costs a lot of money. Buy a cup of coffee for your friend, stay late and help a colleague finish the project. Clean the kitchen to give your spouse a night off, take time to give a compliment to brighten somebody's day. Those small acts cost very little.

Scripture says, "As we have opportunity, let us do good to all people" (Gal. 6:10). Don't miss opportunities to be a blessing. If you hear a coworker talking about how they have to take their car into the shop, consider offering a ride to work the next morning. You're on the lookout for ways you can help. You notice your son's teammate's baseball shoes are worn out. Tell that person, "Let's go up to the store after practice. I want to buy you some new cleats." Maybe you hear your friends who have a new baby talking about how tired they are, how they haven't slept much. Don't say, "Oh yeah, I remember those days. That's really hard." Be sensitive—that's an opportunity to be a blessing. You could say, "How about my spouse and I come over one evening. We'll babysit, and you guys go out to dinner and have some fun."

Open your heart of compassion and look for ways that you can be good to people.

Sometimes it's as simple as listening to someone. I've found that many times if I'm just willing to listen to people, it can help start the healing process for them. When people have a lot of wounds and pain bottled up inside, they need a way to get it out. Some people don't have anybody they believe cares about them or they've been hurt so badly that they struggle to trust anyone. If you will step up and show them a heart of compassion and be their friend by providing a listening ear, you can help them get the heavy load off their chest. It's not about being a counselor or having all the answers to their questions. Just be willing to listen. Take time to show you're concerned for them.

To be on the lookout doesn't mean you have to do big things all at once, but follow the small steps of compassion that God puts in your heart. Those small steps can lead you on a journey that truly changes hearts and transforms lives, including your own.

Every opportunity you have, be good to people.

You may not know why God has put them in your path, but you can be assured it's not a coincidence. God is strategically placing people in your life and trusting you to show them His love. Now it's time to do your part. To be exceptional means you understand God's call on your life. Love well.

—— ⁓⁕⁓ ——

EXCEPTIONAL YOU

I Declare

I will take the time and look for that
something special about every person I meet
and spread deposits of encouragement to them
through simple compliments and kind words.

I will change the atmosphere in my home
by choosing to love well. I will observe the
good things in my family and encourage
them. I will cheer them on and keep a
positive attitude regardless of what is going
on in their life.

I will look for ways to bring the love of God,
healing, and wholeness to people through
my words and actions.

I will be a part of a community of faith
where we love one another, serve one
another, and comfort one another.

I will look for opportunities to be good to
people. I will remember that one simple act
of kindness can turn another person's life
around.

Power Up

Several years ago, I went to a play with some friends at the Wortham Theater here in Houston. Our seats were near the back, making it difficult to see or hear the actors. Unfortunately, we had only one pair of binoculars to share between the five of us, so we took turns using them. When I didn't have them, I felt totally disconnected from the action and found it difficult to follow the story. When my turn would come to use the binoculars, I would draw them up to my eyes, focus in, and suddenly I would feel like I was a part of the story. I could see the expressions on the actors' faces, and I could hear them better because I knew which actor was speaking. With the binoculars, I felt like I was onstage with them. What was once far away had been drawn close.

The apostle Paul says, "But now in Christ Jesus you who once were far away have been brought near by the blood of Christ" (Eph. 2:13). You may have felt far away from God at times during your life, but He always has you in His sights. God has His binoculars focused on you. He is in your story. We just have to realize that He is as close as the very breath that we breathe. Any distance between us and God has been closed through Jesus.

To live your exceptional life, come close to Him so you can be reminded who you really are, His beloved child. Just like at the end of a school day, when your kids may climb into your lap to tell you about the good and bad that happened while you were separated, God is your loving Father and wants you to crawl into His lap. He knows all that you've been through but He still wants you to draw near.

Many people think they need to change their lives before they come to God. But we can't clean up our own lives. We can't bring the change that God wants to bring in our lives. God had to come to us through Jesus. As the apostle Paul said, "While we were still sinners, Christ died for us" (Rom. 5:8). Only Jesus Christ can change your life. There's no mess that you've made that He can't help you clean up. There is nothing that God cannot do for you. There's nothing inside you that would make you distant from God. In Jesus, you are made right with God. He loves you just the way you are, and He came to you just the way you are.

Whatever you're facing today, don't let anything stand between you and God. No matter what you feel or what you've done, He wants a relationship with you. God wants you to know: "I'm right here with you. I'm an up-close-and-personal God and I want to be in your story."

Up Close and Personal

The Bible tells many stories of just how up close and personal God wants to be. Jesus and His disciples were traveling from Judea to Galilee, when Jesus made an unexpected announcement. He said,

"I have to go through Samaria." This statement surprised His disciples because, although Samaria was on the way to Galilee, at that time the Jewish people took the long way around Samaria in order to avoid the Samaritans. The disciples didn't understand why Jesus would break with tradition. Unknown to the disciples, Jesus had a divine appointment with a Samaritan woman.

Around noon, this Samaritan woman walked up to the village well with her watering jar. Most of the other women in the village came to the well in the morning when it was cooler, but this woman waited until noon—the hottest part of the day—in order to avoid the others. In the story we discover that she was a woman who had a bad reputation. So she chose to come to the well alone to avoid the rejection and ridicule of the others.

When she arrived this day, she found Jesus waiting for her. He asked her for a drink of water. She could tell that Jesus was a Jew and was surprised that He would not only associate with her, a Samaritan, but also that He would drink water that she drew from the well.

This woman wanted to stay isolated in her shame, but Jesus had come to draw her near. As He continued to speak to her, she carefully eased a little closer and began to listen to what He was saying. After inquiring about her life, He revealed to her that He already knew everything about her. He knew that she had been married five times and that she was currently living with a man who was not her husband.

That day, Jesus drew close to a woman filled with shame who was living out a multitude of bad choices, and He offered her salvation. She came to draw water to quench her thirst that day. Jesus offered her "living water" that would quench her thirst forever. She felt the incredible closeness of a personal God Who was saying, "I know everything about you—every sin, every mistake, every bad choice—yet, I still love you."

This is what I love about Jesus. Just like He told His disciples, "I need to go through Samaria," He "needed" to come to us and give His life for us. He broke protocol to get to the Samaritan woman, and He broke through every barrier to get to us.

God hasn't brought us close because we're doing

things right. He comes to us to offer us salvation. The beautiful part is that we can receive Him just as we are. Our faults, mistakes, and wrongdoings don't drive Him away; they draw Him closer. He's offering the living water of eternal life, and all we have to do is say yes and receive it freely.

There is another interesting part to the story. Jesus chose this woman to be the first person to whom He would reveal His identity as the Messiah. He had yet to tell anyone, not even His close disciples, that He was the Son of God. Yet, this woman at the well, who had brought upon herself shame and dishonor, was found worthy in the eyes of Jesus to be the first to know Him in a way that no one else did.

The psalmist says, "The LORD is close to the brokenhearted and saves those who are crushed in spirit" (Ps. 34:18). He doesn't shun you, criticize you, or look at what you're doing wrong. He won't throw His hands up and walk away just because you make a mistake. Instead, He draws near to you in love. Even in your worst times, He will offer you His living water. He is drawing near to you even now. Let go of the shame and every negative label that people have put on you, and believe that He is the One Who desires to draw near to you, to heal your broken heart, and to fill your thirsty soul.

You're a Child of the Promise

Whenever I read the stories of Jesus' interactions with different people, I am always amazed by how He treated everyone as significant and valued, how He seemed to see people with different eyes, worthy of His undivided love and attention.

Jesus was teaching in a synagogue on the Sabbath. There was a large crowd gathered around Him, listening intently to His words. Suddenly, He stopped speaking and took notice of one solitary woman among them. She wasn't beautiful or flamboyant or dazzling in any way. The Bible says she "had been crippled by a spirit for eighteen years." In fact, she was bent completely forward and could not straighten up. However, Jesus noticed her.

When she came into the synagogue that day, she might have felt completely unnoticed and alone.

Certainly, most people avoided her. But Jesus saw her. In fact, He immediately stopped everything He was doing and called her to come to Him.

As that woman slowly hobbled closer to Jesus, He spoke to her. "Woman, you are set free from your infirmity today. You're free."

Then He touched her, and she immediately stood up straight for the first time in nearly two decades. All those years she'd been looking at the ground. Her world was filled with the images of dirt, rocks, and people's feet. She could probably go an entire day without seeing another person's face. But at that moment, she straightened up and she saw the face of God.

For eighteen years she had felt invisible, like no one saw her. She had felt uncared for. She had felt judged. To others she was the crippled woman, but Jesus saw who she truly was and drew her near. He saw her and called her "a daughter of Abraham." When He called her that, He was calling her a precious Daughter of the Promise who needed and deserved His compassion and love.

When He set her free that day, she was stunned.

I wonder how long it took before she truly realized that she would never be crippled again. When you've lived a certain way for so long, it's hard to believe you can be any other way. Perhaps you've been bent down under a negative attitude for a long time. You don't even realize that you too are a Child of the Promise and that God has already spoken the Word and set you free. He's already freed you from whatever would bind you, but you just don't realize it yet.

The enemy wants to keep you looking down. He doesn't want you to see ahead to a future filled with promise and hope, and he certainly doesn't want you to see the face of your Savior. He doesn't want you to see that you are a precious Child of the Promise.

But God is looking at you. He sees you, loves you, and wants to draw you near.

Inside every one of us is the voice of God. Don't allow life to drown Him out. He is saying, "You are made in My image. You are valuable, you are significant, and you are important. I chose you because I love you."

Sometimes life tries to overpower that still, small voice. Life can get very loud. Unfair things happen.

People talk negatively about us. Somebody walks out of our life. But what really matters is who you are and who God says you are. You may feel insignificant, but God sees you as valuable. He sees you as important. He calls you His masterpiece.

Don't allow anything to bend you over and bind you up. God is calling you forward today. He is saying, "Whom the Son sets free is free indeed."

Connect to the Source

One of the best ways to enter into every day empowered, inspired, and intentional is to begin each day by spending time with God. Before we check in with our text messages and social media, we should check in with God. We should fuel ourselves with His Word, His promises, and His proclamations, and then we'll enter each day with more power. He is our source. He knows what we need. If we are going to be our best and live exceptional, we need to get in a habit of spending time with God every day.

Ephesians 3 says, "I pray that out of his glorious

riches he may strengthen you with power through his Spirit in your inner being, so that Christ may dwell in your hearts" (vv. 16–17). God wants to strengthen you "in your inner being." We have to focus not on the outer, but on the inner. Just like our physical body gets refreshed and reenergized when we sleep at night, we need to take time to strengthen and fuel our inner man. We can spend so much time getting our outer self ready for the day that we forget to get our inner self prepared for each day. And then we wonder why we're stressed out, struggling, and not able to make good decisions and overcome bad habits. It's because we're not taking time to keep our inner self strong.

Our inner man is our identity; it controls how we respond to life, and it shapes our attitudes and thoughts. When we have a strong inner man, it affects our entire life and helps us make good decisions. A strong core helps us hear from God, to get His direction for our life. When we pay attention to this core of who we are, we can move into each day with strength. You may say, "I'm so busy in the mornings. I have to get my kids to school. I am making breakfast and getting lunches ready. It is so hectic. I don't have time to get quiet and strengthen my inner man." You are doing yourself a disservice. You have to take time to feed your inner man every day.

Joel's father used to say, "Some people feed their physical bodies three hot meals a day, but they feed their spirit one cold snack a week." Every day you need to feed your inner man. Think about what you are nourishing yourself with. Reading the Scriptures is nourishing your inner man with spiritual food. Being quiet and thanking God for His goodness is spiritual food. Declaring God's promises over your life feeds the core of who you are. This is how you stir up your faith each and every morning, by feeding your inner man with the food that it craves. Then you can go out and get your kids ready, pack lunches, and you aren't running on empty; you are fueled with faith.

Don't go through your day feeling discouraged when you can start your day off right by thanking God for His blessings and preparing your mind to be productive. Every day get up and thank God for your health, your relationships, your family, and your job. By starting your day this way, your inner man is being nourished. When you align yourself with God, your outlook will become brighter and your attitude more positive. You will have more strength to turn an ordinary day into an exceptional one.

There have been many mornings I've gotten up and felt like I was dragging. I had no joy, no enthusiasm, thinking, *This day is going to be a struggle. I have so much to do.* I've learned when that happens, I don't have to just give in and go through the day lacking enthusiasm. I know more than ever I have to get to my quiet place and get my inner man fed and my faith stirred.

The apostle Paul says, "Be strong in the Lord... empowered through your union with Him" (Eph. 6:10 AMPC). The Amplified Bible version of Jeremiah 29:13 says to require God "as a vital necessity." That means we can't have the attitude, "If I have time, I'll try to do this." We're not going to live exceptional that way. We're not going to be our best if we're not making God a vital part of our life. Think about that word *vital*. That means you can't live without it. You need it. Your life requires it. That's the way we need to look at spending time with God.

Jesus said, "I am the bread of life. I am the living water. If you drink of Me you'll never thirst again." Are you drinking from the living water? That's God's Word, that's praise, that's thanksgiving. Even during the day when things come against us, it's stressful, and you have opportunities to get upset. Take a five-minute break to gather your thoughts and reach out to God. You can pray in your heart, "God, I need Your help. Thank You for Your peace. I'm asking for Your strength." When you do that, you just took a drink. You bring God's presence into your life. You strengthened your inner man.

The Bible says that when our spirit connects with God's Spirit, something incredible happens—we are ignited with the power of Almighty God. The strongest part of you is not your physical body or your emotional realm. The strongest part of you, the eternal part of you, is your spirit, your inner man, the core of who you are. When you connect the strongest part of you with the strongest Force in the universe, there's a powerful transformation that takes place.

When you make God a priority and you take time to stay connected to Him, you will be empowered to overcome challenges, and He will give you His favor and direct your path even in the difficulties of life.

Switch on the Power

Just as a house is wired to fill a house with power but needs that power turned on at the source, you are fully wired today; you just need to turn on the power by turning to God and asking Him to be your source. Ephesians 3 says: To Him who is able to do immeasurably more than all we can ask, think, or imagine, according to the *power* that is at work within us (see v. 20). He wants to give you power to resist temptation, to walk in integrity, and to give you His peace and joy. You can stand firm against the challenges and disappointments that try to weaken you. You have the ability to be a good parent, raise strong families, have successful careers, and be a blessing everywhere you go. But it all starts by plugging in to the source of power.

What I'm asking you to do is not difficult, but it's one of the most important habits you can ever form. If you don't have a regular quiet time, make a decision to start. Don't think it's not doing anything. It's not only keeping your inner man fed, but it is keeping you powered up and setting the tone for the day. God wants to fill you with the dunamis power of Christ. The Greek word *dunamis* is used over a hundred times in the New Testament. It refers to the strength, ability, and power of God. When you connect to God through Jesus, which is the source of power, God will give you His ability beyond what you can ask, think, or imagine.

Learn to get filled up before you go out. Make it a priority. Spending time with God is vital so you can be empowered. For some of you, this may be the only thing that's holding you back. You're talented, you're dedicated, you love God, but you're not being empowered each day. Your inner man is not being refueled and refreshed. Why don't you make these changes? Get up each morning and connect to the power source by spending time with God. Draw strength from Him. Receive His wisdom, receive

His peace, and receive His power. Then you'll be able to go out and fight the good fight of faith. If you do this, you'll come up higher and higher. God will pour out His blessings and favor, and you'll live the exceptional life He has in store for you.

EXCEPTIONAL YOU

I Declare

No matter how far away I feel from God, I will remember God is always drawing me near to Him. He is up close and personal with me. He has closed any distance between us through Christ Jesus.

Even in my worst times, God meets me wherever I am and offers me the living water of salvation. I will drink and He will heal my broken heart and fill my thirsty soul.

I am a Child of the Promise, and I will not allow the conditions of my life to keep me from my position of faith. I will stand up straight and take my position in this

promise: Whom the Son sets free is free
indeed.

I will enter into each day empowered,
inspired, and intentional by spending time
with God. I will set aside time with God as
a vital part of my life.

I won't get so busy with all the other areas
of my life that I neglect my inner man. I
will strengthen the core of who I am by
putting God's Word in my heart and mind.